Travels
with
Tommy

Photo: Annie Lindekugel

TRAVELS with TOMMY
Stories of Life with a Service Dog

Renée Le Verrier

Travels with Tommy
Stories of Life with a Service Dog
© 2017 by Renée Le Verrier.

LIMYoga

http://www.leverrier.com

Honeydew Productions

Library of Congress Control Number: 2017956162

ISBN: 978-0-9853869-3-1

First Edition: September 2017

10 9 8 7 6 5 4 3 2 1

to Lynne

CONTENTS

Preface   1

Introduction *Silver & Gold*   5

Part ONE

Communication   Let's Talk   11

1. Bad Stove   12

2. Look at That: Three Tales   16

3. Back Up   21

Paws for a Moment *Going Up*   *25*

Paws for a Moment *Name That Tag*   *27*

Fraud Spot *Expandable Leash*   *29*

Part TWO

Respect   Let Me   31

4. Still Talking   33

5. Puddle Jumping   38

6. Basket Half Full   40

Paws for a Moment *Spaghetti*   *43*

Paws for a Moment *The Dremel Incident* 45

Fraud Spot *Four on the Floor*   *48*

Part THREE

Companionship   Let's Go   51

7. Vested Interest   53

8. Music   55

9. Don't Think about It   58

Paws for a Moment *Stuff It*   62

Paws for a Moment *To Sir*   65

Fraud Spot *Look Here*   68

Note *On Companionship*   *71*

Afterword *What Next?*   *73*

Resources   76

About the Author   83

Preface

On a recent flight to Minneapolis, the man in the aisle across from me had taken so many pictures of Sir Thomas, lying at my feet the entire time, he started showing them to other passengers. From airports, conferences, taking in tourist sights, Sir T's image has been captured by cell phones around the world. He's regal. He's well-behaved. He drools, he poops, he cannot function without his dinner and he's terrified of the nail clipper.

Strangers don't see those sides of him. Sometimes the drool runs so thick and long that if he shakes off, it wraps around his nose. Occasionally, cleaning up after him requires two plastic bags. And every now and again, a curtain moves all by itself and he puddles into a quivering mass of fear.

Indeed, no one else sees the pillar he can also be, literally. I've risen from the carpet, driveway, garage floor, feet of snow, parking lots, and pine-needle-strewn trails in the woods by wrapping my arms around him to hoist myself to a kneeling position before leaning all my weight on him to stand back up.

While I jokingly refer to him as the combination of a toddler and date, needing me as well as wanting to be with me, there is no comparison to other relationships. No one else has been by my side 24/7. I adore my husband, but he doesn't accompany me to the bathroom and I don't always check if he has fresh water. There is no comparison to living with a service dog. But there are certainly stories.

To divide these stories anecdotally, into a chronology or by location would give only a partial account of living with a service dog. He is a part of me and I a part of him. We are partners. A solid partnership is built on communication, respect and companionship.

In Part One, Communication runs through each story. Part Two highlights Respect and Part Three focuses on Companionship with a service dog partner. I sprinkle in some quick tales and sidebars about fraud service dog teams—an increasingly common practice that is disrupting and disturbing.

Dog people share a common bond. We approach one another when one of our pets is present. We especially take to another dog when we're on holiday or otherwise away from our own family friend. Our canines can make us feel loved, understood, happy, and we readily reach out to pet, go nose-to-nose with, or simply coo over another person's pet. And, we reciprocate for someone who needs a dog fix from the furry companion at the end of someone else's leash.

Since service dogs are not pets, the common bond is broken, interrupted by the word *service* in front of *dog*. Service dog partners share love and happiness but we also share a dependence upon one another to do a job and do it well. Our experiences are not those of an owner and pet, they are of having eyes, ears, legs through our dogs. They are amazing dogs whose stories should be told, but not by interrupting them at the market or airport.

Which is why I share a few here, complete with a couple of pictures.

Introduction

Silver & Gold

Littermates dozed in a heap of round bellies and giant paws. Except for Lola. She stood and watched me. Her gray eyes were set in a serious silver face. The combination made her seem less like a pup and more like someone's nana— a nana who listens, even to the unspoken words. I imagined I could tell her anything. I figured she probably already knew anything I'd tell her. I decided I was in love.

Meeting Lola marked my initial visit to a farm that raises and trains Great Danes as mobility service dogs. The organization had reviewed my application and invited me for an interview and tour. I lived close enough to drive down.

By the time I exited onto a road that meandered past ponds and cornfields to a giant red mailbox, I felt I was far, far away. The driveway led uphill to a gate where a volunteer waved me in. He pointed to where I'd find the trainers, a vast variety of chickens and, of course, the puppies. It was my first encounter with service dogs and the first step on my journey with one.

On my next visit, I sought out the silver girl. She readily trotted over to me and stood for a moment as if reading my mind. Every woman's dream, I thought, someone who understands me. I calculated how I could wait eighteen to twenty-four months for the four-legged cane I needed sooner.

A trainer supplied the answer before I got the chance to ask the question aloud. She showed me several kennels that housed the leaner, taller pups I hadn't met yet. They had grown out of the roly-poly stage and into training. Their next level of preparation for partnership involved working with their human.

Among them stood Thomas. Just a year, he was the first born of nine siblings. Seven were the same-size and coloring—black-and-white mantels, the kind of markings that made them look as though they wore tuxedos. They all looked alike to me.

When they darted outside to romp together, I had no idea which one was Thomas. The trainer pointed him out again. He did have one distinctive feature that differentiated him from the others: his eyes. They drooped in a saggy, sleepy way. I looked into those eyes and he looked away.

I can wait for the silver girl to grow up, I thought.

But it wasn't up to me. And even though the trainer listed Thomas's many attributes, summing up his qualifications with, "He's such a good boy," it wasn't up to her, either.

These partnerships, I discovered, aren't arranged unions determined by matching up forms and paper clipping them together. They begin more like a date, where an early spark, if tended to and nurtured, grows into warm flames. Some don't blossom, even the love-at-first-sight meetups, like in human relationships.

The next time I saw Thomas, I brought a brush in the hopes of enticing him to look at me. The date analogy would be that I wore a nice dress and makeup, though I stood in faded jeans as I held out the brush to show him. He edged toward me. I waited. As he edged closer, I glanced down and noticed his feet. His matching littermates each had four white socks— black legs with snowy paws. Thomas had three socks, but his right foreleg was different. It had a whole stocking of white from above his elbow down to his toes.

Hey, my legs don't match, either, I told him. *They're two different sizes from my stroke.* He set his bloodshot gaze on me for a second. He turned away again. But, when he did, he also took a full step towards me. That one step became two. I placed a hand on his shoulder and brushed. That right leg of his cracked open the door between us.

Our training started and we were together often. During that time, I told him about where I lived, that he'd like the yard and nearby woods. He stood close and listened. When I didn't talk, he didn't hear me. Anything I spoke aloud, however, he understood and did whatever I asked of him. Like the trainer had said, He's such a good boy.

One afternoon, I looked him in the eyes and explained what I needed from him if we were to commit to this relationship. I described how

Parkinson's is finicky and inconsistent, that the switch from walking the dog to walking with the help of the dog could be instant and not always graceful. He didn't turn away. The next time I dropped him back at the farm after our training, he leapt back into my car.

We've grown on each other since the brush date. We've certainly grown with each other. He taught me that he couldn't boldly look me in the eye the way Lola did early on because he needed to see who I really was first. I know he'll never be intuitive, foretelling my mood or predicting my needs. It's not the dog he is. He will, however, do whatever I ask of him, except get out of the car without me.

Silver was not for me. Instead, I seem to have struck gold.

PART ONE

Communication

Let's Talk

Yes, I talk to my dog. Quite often and all throughout the day. It's in his nature—it's at the core of his being—to be a good boy. He'll do whatever I ask of him. But he can be good only if what I ask is clear. So I talk to him. And he listens. He was trained to listen. But he tells me things, too, and I've had to learn how to listen.

1

Bad Stove

Near the end of our formal training together, before we were officially a team, Sir Thomas came for a visit. The trainer brought him to my house for an official "Home Visit." This inspection was an essential part of the process of transitioning Sir T from the agency that raised and trained him into my home. Our home.

"C'mon in," I'd called from the sink when I heard the knock. I'd just finished putting away the last of the breakfast dishes. Not that a few bowls in the sink would disqualify me as a good handler, but I wanted everything to be neat, tidy, just right.

The door opened and Thomas sprang across the tile, skidded to a stop and lowered his chin to rest it on the counter top. He might have looked downright regal if, first, his entry hadn't been quite so goofy and, second, if he hadn't chosen the spot right beside the stove top. Being a silly boy and being face level with flaming rings is not a good combination, I thought.

Fortunately, the burners were all off. It was also fortunate that the trainer shooed him away in an instant. That gave me—his almost-human—the chance to greet him in his almost-home with praises and pats rather than a stern voice and pointed finger. There would need to be some rules set soon, however, regarding proximity of that handsome face to those burn-ers.

"How do you keep your guys away from the stove?" I knew the trainer had three Danes of her own at home.

"Simple," she shrugged. "I don't cook."

Oh, I thought. But I do.

She offered to help come up with a plan af-ter she completed her assessment. With a mea-suring tape and forms in-hand, she wandered in and out with an eye to safety, room for a large dog bed, exercise space and fence height.

Meanwhile, I considered the kitchen. It was the room where I spent most of my time. The room where I'd need my service dog the most. The room with the stove.

Throughout our training together, I learned a great deal about Sir T. What topped the list—and still does—is his embodiment of a Great Dane phrase: gentle giant. He's as sensitive as he is big. Whisper in his ear—the news, a bad poem—and he'll wag and wag. Raise my voice—in a discussion about politics or out of frustration that I'm still on hold with the insurance company—and he cringes. I could whisper my frustrations and shout out praise, he'd still respond to the tone of my voice over the words I spoke.

So, I'd heard that by scolding the item rather than the dog, the effect is the same. 'Loud voice equals bad thing hence steer clear of bad thing' was the logic. I figured, why not test this theory?

I stood by in the doorway while the trainer was measuring outside. He stepped up beside me. When I ventured into the kitchen, he followed. Easing toward the stove, he was still at my side. I turned to place all my attention on the front two burners. With finger pointing, I bent toward that very bad stove and told it so in a very stern voice.

"Bad stove. Bad. Bad, bad stove."

Out of the corner of my eye, I saw it. Tommy was slinking away with 'I don't want to be associated with that bad stove, I'm outta here' written down his spine all the way to his tucked tail. Before he got too far, I turned all my attention on him and in a happy, whispery voice I told him what a very good boy he was. His tail untucked and wagged.

My house inspection passed easily and Sir Thomas moved in a month later. We've been partners for years. He has yet to go near the stove.

2

Look at That

From restaurants to quick-marts, wherever Sir Thomas and I go, people talk. About dogs. I can't help but overhear these canine conversations when I'm seated or standing nearby. Whatever discussions were taking place before we stepped in, they merge towards one theme.

Mostly, the dog talk revolves around family pets present and past. Some focus on a breed and a handful of others discuss aspects of service dogs. It makes me smile that there exists a commonality—the topic of dogs—that weaves us all together.

Sometimes, there are loose strands in that dogdom fabric. One morning, Thomas and I passed several pockets of small crowds browsing the goods at neighborhood yard sales. As we passed one, I noticed a couple turn their attention from the brass lamp on the lawn to the dog walking beside me. I heard the woman wondering aloud if that was a Great Dane. The man answered with a knowing tone, "Yes." And just as confidently, he added, "But it's a miniature Great Dane."

I think even Tommy giggled at that.

There are other times when the threads that tie us get a tad twisted up. One afternoon, on my way home from errands, I took the long way so I could pass my favorite bakery. It was the time of day that begged for an energy boost. Not that I needed any convincing. The aromas, the shelves and baskets and racks of crusty breads, even the windows were right out of a patisserie in Paris. Stopping in boosted my whole day.

I decided on my order in the parking lot. Going inside without a plan would have been like going to an auction without first setting a limit on how high you'll go for that antique side table that would look so perfect in the front hall. Each loaf, each pastry was that perfect.

With Tommy at my side, we approached the berry tarts and almond croissants and pecan swirls. I could hear the conversations around me shift to dog talk. I ordered a half dozen cookies—chocolate chunk,with Belgian dark chocolate and like none I've ever made—to take home, with maybe an extra for the drive.

At a table in a far corner, I heard the familiar, "Mom, look at that big dog!" I glanced over and saw several young children and three women. As the cashier rang up my order and I sorted through my wallet for the amount, I could hear one of the women explaining that he was a "helper dog." She added, "He's helping that lady see."

If I had been closer, I might have smiled at the kids and let them ask questions. That way they could learn that not all service dogs are guide dogs.

Instead, I felt the kids watching Tommy help me out to the parking lot. How I'd have enjoyed overhearing what the woman told the kids when they saw me get in the driver's seat.

Wherever we go, people comment on how big Sir Thomas is, often comparing him to a horse, as in, "That's not a dog, it's a horse" or "You could put a saddle on him."

Even though the comments stem from well-meaning, friendly folk, I sometimes ignore them. As fresh and clever as it seems to the speaker, I've heard it many times. On one occasion, a particularly fresh strand threaded into the tapestry.

It was an August afternoon and I was playing the role of tour guide for visiting family. To help entertain my son, who'd long since tired of the town's historic houses and harbor-side cafes, I gave him a pencil and pad to keep a Tommy tally. He made two columns: *H* for horse comments and *S* for saddle remarks.

Downtown was busy, which kept him occupied but nearby while I and his aunt drifted from shop to shop. We talked each other into getting a hat. She chose a floppy, striped beach-style chapeau that gave her a carefree look with flair. For me, it was between a rather dignified Panama-like hat and the wilder, wide-brimmed straw one that would've gone well with boots and spurs. I opted for the wild one.

Donning our new hats, we reconvened on the boardwalk with the rest of the family. As we gazed out at the boats, a woman behind us said, "Honey, look at the big dog."

There was a pause. Then a little girl's voice, "Momma," she said. "I want to be a cowgirl."

She convinced me that size does matter. But not when singled out. She saw that his size is related to mine, that from my toes all the way to the top of my hat, Tommy and I go together.

3

Back Up

At the end of his middle school band concert, my son needed to collect his sheet music and saxophone. I waited in a hallway overflowing with parents and grandparents. I was in the midst of a waning meds spell and felt a bit like I was inside a pinball game being bumped from every angle. Sir Thomas was working that much harder to make up for my non-working balance and keep me upright in the crowd.

A very tall man stepped toward us, one hand on his video camera, the   other outstretched. Like in airports, markets, post offices, cafes, museums, the hand reached for Sir Thomas. We had seen them all: little hands, wrinkly, hairy and gloved. This man's hand, however, was quite large.

Sir Thomas, in his vest and collar, sported a number of DO NOT PET patches. The man must have seen his SERVICE DOG and IGNORE ME messages in bold lettering because he was filming them.

The man moved closer. I tightened my grip on Thomas's harness and directed my firm yet polite voice toward him.

"No, thank you." I said. "He's working."

The video cam and hand continued to close in.

"No," I said louder. "Please don't pet."

Thomas stopped. I stopped. The man continued toward us.

If he reaches my Dane, I thought, the effect will be the same as kicking my cane out from under me. With the desire to remain vertical, I hissed, "BACK OFF."

The man lowered his camera and appeared quite stunned.

It took Tommy a day to calm down.

A great many more hand encounters later, I realized that I'd been wrong all along. Oh, the

Do Not Pet rule still holds. Hands are distracting. In fact, I had allowed those wriggling fingers distract me.

To do his job, Thomas takes his cues from me. Each time I directed my "No, thank you" to a stranger, I was no longer communicating with Thomas. But he was still listening. And what he heard was tension and frustration and No. He knew that I was unhappy but could not help me because I gave him no cues. For him to do his job, I realized, I need to do mine: maintain communication with him.

So now when I encounter hands, I simply keep my focus on Tommy. Since it's not his action needing correction, I don't say No to him. I give him something to do, not something not to do.

"Back up," I say.

He backs up.

I say, "Good boy."

He wags.

When strangers reach again, I ask Thomas to back up again.

Even if people can't read his DO NOT PET patches, when the dog and his human keep backing away, they eventually get the message.

Paws for a Moment

Going Up

I taught a yoga class for years at a busy hospital in Boston. There was a popular parking garage nearby where there was always a space, but sometimes not until the seventh floor. Had I noticed the elevator's glass-walled cars, I might have had time to turn Sir Thomas around to back him on.

But I was too late. The door flapped open and Tommy's eyes widened. He bent all four legs into a crouch and froze. Elevators had never frightened him; he was actually quite comfortable on them. A fallen leaf rustling in the wind, however, now that was spooky. So, too,

I learned, was seeing that rustling leaf from the elevator.

I turned to see what he saw. From his level, stepping onto the elevator looked as though he'd be stepping off of the planet. I was not even going to try to make him. Besides, taking the stairs gave us both a chance to get some exercise.

Paws for a Moment

Name that Tag

After five-plus years, I continue to be taken aback when strangers see Sir Thomas and me, acknowledge that they've read the various Do Not Pet, Mobility Dog, Ignore Me, Don't Distract I'm Working tags and patches and, yet, they still ask his name. Ninety-nine percent of the time, it's a friendly request made out of genuine curiosity.

My hesitation in answering stems from that one percent who'll then call out his name. It takes only one distraction to send me to crashing into the avocado display at the grocery store or face-plant onto the floor at the Delta check-in counter.

For safety's sake—mine—I often respond with a smile and a fake name. Today, while enjoying a breakfast-served-all-day lunch with my husband and our son, Tommy dutifully napped on his mat beside our table. A couple stepped in and as they passed by, I sensed their pace slowing.

"Aww." I heard. I knew The Question was coming. I couldn't answer as I'd just taken a bite of my omelet.

The woman murmured to herself, "What's his name?" She leaned in close and scanned his patches and tags for the answer.

"Ah, " she said, standing back up. "Service Dog," she said to her partner.

"Service Dog?" she said again in a questioning, what-kind-of-name is that tone.

"Oh," she said next. "Service Dog. Oh."

They scurried off, leaving the three of us laughing over our eggs. Tommy went back to sleep.

Fraud Spot

Expandable Leash

From airports to theaters, cafes to markets, service dogs must be with their humans to be of service. That can mean staying beside the person to steady, walking in front to guide or standing behind to alert. The dog focuses on the same task as the handler. Communication between the two is essential. Service dogs are the legs, the ears and more of that human,. None of these should scamper ahead to sniff and frolic. Service dogs are attached to their disabled partners like an appendage.

If Spot sports a vest and also a retractable leash, odds are they're accessories. He is not working (and neither is their disguise).

PART TWO

Respect

Let Me

If communication is the key to a strong relationship, respect is what keeps the door open when we can't find that key. Initially, Sir T and I needed to learn about each other's quirks and how to live with them. With time, we've come to hold them dearly.

When anything from a foolishly sentimental greeting card to memories of my late sister cause me to tear up, for example, Sir T often sleeps through it. He knows that I'm a crier and there's nothing he can do or that I expect him to do about it. If, however, I'm physically stuck and cry out in frustration, he's on alert.

I know that Sir T needs me to let him outside to do what we call "his business." I also know that I need to let him out less frequently when raindrops are a certain size. No one explained this or trained us on these nuances. Sometimes, there are no words.

4

Still Talking

All through elementary school, I was a talker. I talked before class. During class. Walking to class. Walking to my newly assigned seat in back of the class, to which I was sent for talking.

Oh, if only I could step back in time to the teachers who darkened my mostly-A report cards with their Conduct: Cs. I would gather those Scrooges of verbal communication in a classroom for a workshop on how vocabulary and grammar skills directly affect walking skills.

Talk to Walk Workshop

Welcome to a day in the life of a service dog team.

Pre-workshop Observational Opportunities

Note the bond between dog and human, well before the working vest gets strapped on, through eye contact, tail wagging, smiles (human and dog) and continual talk. Includes:

• Morning handler-canine stretches and giant multisyllabic yawns.

• Other start-the-day routines include ear scratches and tickle time along with interspersed utterings of "Yes, I love you. You know I love you."

Learning Objectives

Gain the importance of talk in the service dog partnership through a better understanding of:

• Vocabulary: How handlers use their words during morning, afternoon and evening routine tasks.

Example: Though I go from the bedroom into the kitchen each morning to make tea, I don't say *kitchen* to Tommy. It's an endpoint, but much can happen en route. I could lose my balance, need to turn back, take a quick right for the bathroom. His job is to help ensure each step I take is successful. So, our morning jaunt might sound more like this: *Step, step*. If his pace isn't quite with mine: *Ease, I'm creaky this morning*. Stop: *Whoa*. Wait, I'm going to pick up that lone sock I'll point to it so he knows where I'm aiming. *Brace, okay I have it, step forward. Left. Whoa.* (I enter the laundry room, tossed sock into basket.) *Thank you. Now, right, still right, right* (we're turning around). *Good, and forward.* In the evening, however, when something is on the stove boiling over, I need a direct line to the kitchen. That would sound more like this: *Forward. Let's go!*

• Grammar: Why and when handlers choose two-word phrases, run-on sentences or mono-syllabic affirmations.

Vocabulary doesn't stand alone. Interwoven with my choice of words is how to best string them together so that my verbal guidance translates to his physical guidance. Sir T can't possibly read my mind or my body cues to know what I'll need in each step. That depends on factors such as my awareness of what I'll need in each step, which depends on such things as when I took my meds and if there's an obstacle to navigate around. (To a person with Parkinson's, an obstacle can be a doorway, a scrap of paper on the floor, a breeze or a stray sock that belongs in the laundry room.)

Q & A / Discussion

Please pose your questions at this time. The handler must focus to determine and verbalize what she needs so the service dog understands what he needs to do. Interrupting the team at work breaks the concentration required for successful task performance.

Breaks

Note that talk is essential for the service dog team during breaks and you may overhear them in the restroom. Breaks are generous as and they allow time for canines to assist their humans to the restroom as well as time and space for humans to let their canines outside for a break.

Refreshments

Available throughout the day. Do not feed a service dog. Please note that dog cookies are reserved for handlers only, to be offered to canines by handlers at handler's discretion. A cookie is worth a thousand words.

Summary

Please feel free to share this information. You've always been good teachers. I believed it to be so even as a kid, which I would've said if I'd been allowed to talk a bit more.

5

Puddle Jumping

When I mentioned in the *Introduction* that Thomas would do anything I asked of him, I may have stretched the truth. Yes, he has accompanied me on outings he'd rather not have. Good boy that he is, he settles down beside me on his mat even when the dentist pokes whirring, whining instruments in my mouth. And, only once did he pop up from the floor-rattling thuds and grunts of boxing classes. In retrospect, the minivan on that Caribbean island we squeezed seven humans into before I asked him to load up probably shouldn't have been mini. My brave Sir Thomas would do anything I ask. Anything but step through a puddle.

Puddles, apparently, are disturbingly dark crevasses capable of swallowing up a giant dog, say, the size of a Great Dane. He'd side-step, dance around, over or across the street and back to avoid one. I did not know this when Thomas first came home with me. And, some-how, our training sessions together occurred in fair weather only.

I knew of his agility at work and at play. His footwork actually earned him several nick-names. When artfully prancing at-ease, he be-came Tommy Lautrec. His figure-eights around the yard at full speed dubbed him Tommy the Train and his ability to pivot and spring straight into the air made him Tommy-loo.

Ever since the doctor's appointment, to which I arrived late, sodden and more dishev-eled than I could blame on Parkinson's, my four-legged cane has yet another name: Tommy Tallulah. Tallulah is Native American for 'leap-ing waters.'

Picture a harness with a handle attached to a human. Imagine those long legs leaping over each pool of rain water with his human along for the ride. The result is, I, too, now sidestep around puddles. It's not much to ask given all I ask of him.

6

Basket Half Full

Unlike Sir Thomas, I have never been a good sleeper. He curls up on his bed and is into full-body dreaming twitches before I've even fluffed my pillow. He whoops and snores throughout the night. He doesn't wake me, I hear him because I'm already awake. The window of time I'm most often wide-eyed is when it is no longer night but still pre-dawn. The witching hour.

For years, I investigated diet, bedtimes, pillows, mattresses, exercise, lighting fixtures, lotions. I tried replacing the night stand clock. I even stuffed it into my sock drawer. No change.

One night when my husband was away on business, my son at camp and Tommy, well, he was asleep. The house was mine, I thought. In the past, I'd wander about tending to chores. It felt better knowing that if I wasn't getting my sleep, at least I was getting my to-do list completed.

"Be right back, Tommy," I whispered.

He sighed and I shuffled toward the laundry room.

I miscalculated a left turn, reached my hand out for the edge of the doorway for support and missed. I did manage to twist mid-plunge and landed backside first rather than head first into a laundry hamper.

A small pile of sheets padded my landing. They'd also molded into the form of the basket, which had molded around my backside. The basket and I were one, making it impossible to try to tip myself over and roll out. I soon saw that hoisting myself up wasn't an option either because I couldn't reach the washing machine or any shelves.

Tricky time, that witching hour. Its 4:00-am energy shot made me forgot that I no longer moved very well in the middle of the night.

Maybe it wasn't forgetfulness but denial. Parkinson's was referred to in our house as the "P-word" during the early years of my diagnosis and *disability* just didn't sound good in any sentence.

There was no denying, however, that I was in a predicament that grew more uncomfortable and more serious with each witching hour moment. I was alone in the house, nowhere near a phone, in need of meds and a bathroom, stuck on the floor wedged into a laundry basket.

And Tommy appeared.

Paws for a Moment

Spaghetti

"Left. Good. Forward." We turned down the Pasta and Sauces aisle.

"Whoa. And, Brace." Tommy stopped beside the cart and let me lean on him so I could get a jar of sauce. I noticed a man standing with his back to us. I figured he didn't see us, so I plotted a path around him to get to a box of spaghetti.

"Step back," I said, "back, and right."

I turned and nearly slammed into the man's back. Again, I asked Tommy to step back. The man stepped back. Tommy stepped back.

"Whoa!" They both halted.

"Side step left three times."

Tommy didn't move. I didn't expect him to because that's not a command he knows. The man, however, shifted far enough to the side that he could see me. He looked quite surprised to see a dog with me. I thanked him, reached for two boxes of spaghetti noodles and said to Tommy, "Step forward."

Paws for a Moment

The Dremel Incident

Since all eyes land on Sir Thomas when we're out in the community, I take his grooming seriously. My hair, on the other hand, tends toward that 'windswept' look (a.k.a. 'uncombed') or gets tucked under any variety of hats (especially when 'windswept' leans toward 'witchy'). As for my nails, there's typically a leftover mix of ochre and cadmium red paint from a project.

Sir Thomas, however, leaves the house glossed and trimmed. Admittedly, he's a handsome guy to start. But after a few brush strokes, he shines. There's a healthy luster along his back as well as an inner glow from our one-on-one, hands-on time. He loves it, leans into it, groans contented groans.

Toenails are a different story. If a pair of clippers lurks somewhere in the room, he knows it, slinks away from it, quivers in a mass of drool. He'd had a nail cut too short in his puppy days and the memory clearly lives on.

To keep his claws this side of talons and reduce the trauma of trimming, I tried a Dremel. I'd never heard of one until a friend suggested it. A power tool? For toenails? Really?

First, I switched it on to its lowest setting and moved about the house with it in hand. My plan was to desensitize Tommy to the potentially scary hum. Did this a few times. No quivering. Hmmm, this may work.

Next, I sat near him and filed my own nails. Did this for a couple of days. No slinking.

When I powered up the Dremel and pressed it against his nails, he tolerated the vibration for a whole front paw. Impressive. When I leaned in to work on the next set of nails, I learned an important lesson: Take Tommy's grooming seriously. Take power tools more seriously.

I'd blame the mishap on my Parkinson's, but it had more to do with my hair. Add a power-tool novice to loose strands of 'windswept' hair. Next, lean in for close work with this long-stemmed, hand-held machine that whirs in a tight circular motion. The result: Yelp! Not from Tommy, but from me.

The Dremel snatched my hair and wound itself tight until it spun against my skull. My hand still gripped it, my thumb searching for the 'off' button. Once I found it, the only way to get the tool out was with a scissors. Needless to say, I wore a hat for a few days after the Dremel incident. Oh, and from now on, I'll be wearing one every time I groom Sir Thomas. Or maybe I can go back to the clippers and hum while I trim.

Fraud Spot

Four on the Floor

In addition to a high level of training, service dogs undergo temperament scrutiny from as early on as their puppy days. They must prove not only that they can guide, alert and steady their humans, they must also show they can settle into standby mode. Once the service has been done—such as providing the stability and support for their human going to a restaurant—the dog goes into a lengthy down-stay. This can be under or beside the table and lasts until service is needed again.

To do so, all paws remain on the floor. I bring a mat for Tommy, both because he has boney elbows and because it puts a layer between him and the dirty floor. *Standby* means not up on a lap or chair. No sitting in the booth, eating off the table, playing catch with the admiring children from another table. All real situations of some not-real service dogs. All real situations of some service dog graduates, too, whose handlers missed out on highly important training.

The best compliments I've received regarding Sir Thomas have come from nearby diners who notice him for the first time as I rise to leave and he stands to assist me: "I didn't know there was a dog in here." My service dog provides me with the brain message-to-legs link that Parkinson's has dissolved. He's not my Get Out of Jail Free card for common courtesy or common sense.

PART THREE

Companionship

Let's Go

Service dogs, as defined by the Americans with Disabilities Act (ADA), provide work or tasks for people with disabilities. Their training paves the way to team work with a human. The team's ongoing communication and respect strengthen the capacity for the disabled human to live independently.

It wouldn't be right to leave out mention of the extra bonus that accompanies the service dog's ability: the service dog's personality. We care for our dogs and enjoy being with them.

It's a good thing they can be goofy, grand, or simply good because they're with us 24/7. We love them dearly, but we also really like them.

7

Vested Interest

Tommy's closet contains a variety of vests and harnesses. I use the sturdiest, with its special grip handle for travel, especially through the chaos of airports. His yellow one is much more lightweight, which is good for summer. There's also a trio of soft-strapped pajamas, one each in purple, green and blue.

My favorite is leather with silver studs and buckles both because it highlights Tommy's handsomeness and because there are numerous spaces to add Do Not Pet patches. He was wearing that one while out at a local café. I ran into a woman there I'd met in an art class. She remembered Tommy simply as the well-behaved dog that accompanied me to class. He was always already tucked under the table before she arrived and, to my surprise, she had never noticed his Do Not Pet patches.

She greeted me and gazed at the patches before she cupped both hands under Tommy's chin, brought her face to his, rubbed his ears and gave him a giant hug. "Do Not Pet?" she said, still rubbing his head. "Why, he's the nicest dog I know. He's not going to hurt anyone who tries to pet him!"

8

Music

For years, I lived in a small New England city that hosted an annual chamber music festival each summer. For a week in August, the various old stone churches downtown, with their ideal resonance and intimate settings, transformed into mini concert halls.

The first time I attended the event with Sir Thomas, I learned something new about the architecture of those churches. The information related not to the bell towers or the granite or marble but to the wooden bench-like pews.

We arrived early, while there was still an echo inside. Thomas perked his ears. I could see his nose twitching. He knew he hadn't been inside that church before; those sounds and smells were unfamiliar. I paused to let him take in the setting and gazed around for a place for us.

I'd learned early on that seat selection—from cafes to movie theaters—with Tommy requires its own set of parameters. Best view falls well behind whether getting to it is a straight shot with no twists, turns or blocks in the path (Parkinson's doesn't do twists, turns or blocks) Second, is it out of the way (which usually means there are twists or turns to get to it) of foot traffic to avoid both the attention and, more importantly, a stepped-on tail? And, still superseding view, is there enough room on the floor for Tommy?

I spotted the perfect space and directed Tommy to lead us to it. Together, we made our way to the side with a less-than-perfect view of the piano. I unrolled Tommy's mat and he readily lay down on it knowing he was relieved of his duties for the moment. Feeling relieved of my seat selection duty, I settled in.

The quartet warmed up and Thomas started to doze. Although people had been streaming in, the row in front of us remained empty. Until three elderly women sidestepped into the pew, swooshing their skirts aside to sit. It was then that I became aware of the design of the wooden seating.

The rows of pews were evenly spaced apart by about the width of one Great Dane. As the ladies' behinds made contact with the seat boards, it was clear that the open space between them and the back support was the equal to the height of a Great Dane's large, wet nose.

9

Don't Think about It

Though the words sat inches before my eyes, I didn't notice them at first. I was too busy muttering about the broken traffic signal and heavy-sighing that I'd be late for my yoga class. I gripped the steering wheel and grumbled.

Stuck in a stand-still line of cars and trucks, my vehicle began to move. Up and down, like the quickening beat to a country-rock song. Very much like the heavy breathing of a giant dog.

A glance in the rear-view mirror confirmed it. Tommy—typically in full snore mode in the back of my station wagon—stood in a full-pant. Drool pooled up on the seat cover. I opened the window even though I knew heat wasn't the culprit. He felt uneasy because he could tell that I was.

When he senses stress—most often in my voice—he comes to me. Sometimes, such as the evenings when I talk back to the news, unhappy with the state of things, he sidles up beside me, as though to say, *Here I am. What do you need me to do to help?* Other times, I can be retelling a can-you-believe type of story to my husband, my voice getting impassioned, and Tommy will appear, his head hung low. Those soulful eyes peer up at me seeking reassurance that I'm not leaving, about to keel over, or in any way upset with him.

In the car, he couldn't come to me, which made it even worse. I loosened my grip on the steering wheel and took a deep breath, exhaling it evenly but loud enough for him to hear the calmness of it. I laughed at myself and my silly worry about being late and checked the mirror again. Tommy heard me, sensed the air lighten. He sat. The car stopped bouncing. Before too long, the car in front of me edged forward. That's when I saw the message adorned on its bumper: The sticker read: *Don't Believe Everything You Think.* I thought I'd be late and that being late was the worst thing that could happen. Upsetting him was worse than that. I ended up with minutes to spare but probably would never have made it to class, at least not mentally, if I hadn't stopped believing my worries.

I had to wonder if Tommy snuck out and stuck that bumper sticker it on that car. He takes care of me in so many ways.

And I take care of him. We're like an old couple that way, walking in sync, aware of each other's quirks, leaning and being there to lean on. If I'm walking through the living room and reach my right hand out, I don't need to say anything. He knows he can saunter over for pets and ear scratches. If I'm stepping through the living room and reach my left palm down, he knows he needs to scramble get his shoulders under that hand to stabilize me.

Sometimes, he has to remind me with that particular tilted-head gaze that it's 5:01 and dinner time was at 5:00. Sometimes, if I need his help to get to the food bowl, I have to remind him to walk at my body's pace, not that of his stomach.

The one lone bumper sticker on my car is positioned not on the bumper but in a more visible spot. In the driver's side corner of the back window, it reads: In Case of Emergency, Do Not Separate Service Dog from Handler. It's not a situation I would like to believe would ever happen. But if a traffic jam became a traffic accident, we'll need each other even more. Don't even think about separating us.

Paws for a Moment

Stuff It

I sat with a friend and colleague at a service dog information table in the exhibitor's hall during a full-day Parkinson's conference. Though we're polar opposites on the personality scale—I teach yoga, she shoots skeet—we're often mistaken for each other. Wearing matching service dog T-shirts and each flanked by related Great Danes, passersby could easily have thought they were seeing double. As attendees stopped to ask questions, however, it became clear that there were actually two of us.

We handed out stacks of brochures with ADA Guidelines, FAQs and a list of resources. A small crowd gathered and we took turns answering how our dogs help with balance and demonstrating they step in stride beside us to keep us upright and moving forward.

Several people commented that they thought service dogs were for the visually impaired. It was a pleasure to see the surprised looks and hear the "wows" as our little audience realized the double benefit of a service animal. In addition to providing assistance for what Parkinson's had disabled, that assistance comes in the form of a gentle-giant canine partner.

A woman approached after the crowds had dispersed. I'd noticed her among those who watched the way Tommy leaned to counter my tipping when my balance slipped. She was nearby when my friend spoke to her dog to step back and certainly she heard us both praise our four-legged partners for a job well done.

"I think a service animal would be good for my mother," she said.

I waited, about to clear the last of the brochures from the table.

"She's ninety," the woman continued. "And lives in a nursing home."

My colleague and I glanced at each other.

"She can't feed it or let it outside. Is that important?"

She shifted from one leg to another and added, "She really just needs something fuzzy to pet."

Were I not so exhausted, I might have explained. Instead, what came out of my mouth echoed my colleague's immediate response, a double shot of,

"Yes. Get her one. A stuffed one. Get her a stuffed animal."

Paws for a Moment

To Sir

Strangers often ask me if my service dog ever gets the chance to be, "you know, just a dog?"

If by 'just a dog,' they mean romping and napping and snacking on treats, look at the shine in his coat and the spring in his step for the answer.

If by 'just a dog,' they mean spending his day with his human and never being left behind in the empty house wondering, waiting, he has that hands-down over most pets.

If by 'just a dog,' they mean snoring the night away in a snuggy bed in the same room with his human, most certainly.

Each night, I tuck Sir Thomas into his bed, his favorite fluffies under and around him, and I whisper, Thank You. I want him to know that not only was he a Good Boy all day—he's such a good boy—but also that I appreciate what he does.

On one hand, I expect him to do his job and do it well. He's not 'just a dog,' he's a service dog. He was raised and trained to perform the tasks he does. I remind him what a good boy he is every time he steps in to help me.

My end-of-day gratitude reaches beyond the job at hand, though, the way a beam of sun lights up more than a spot on the carpet. I tuck him in wanting him to know about all the places he warms me and brightens my life. The nights following an especially shining performance on his part, I sing him a goodnight song in my off-key way, borrowed from the aptly named "To Sir with Love:"

> ... *How do you thank a dog*
> *Who has taken you step by step across the room?*
> *It isn't easy, but I'll try*

If you wanted the sky
I would write across the sky in letters
That would soar a thousand feet high
To Sir, with love

...

... how do you tell a dog
who has steadied you, been beside you with
   each reach
grounded you so your soul can fly

If you wanted the moon
I would try to make a star
But I, would rather you let me give my heart
To Sir, with love.

Just a dog? I think not.

Fraud Spot

Look Here

My husband is tall and could easily see over the causeway railing down to the United Air check-in counter. He spotted her a moment before she stepped onto the elevator. I'm tall but my eyes studied the slow path Tommy and I were navigating through the rapids of travelers rushing and bubbling through the terminal. I verbally guided him as he physically led me toward our gate number.

"Wait for it," he said.

I stopped, held tight to Tommy for support and gazed in the direction my husband was looking. The elevator doors dinged open.

A white-haired couple stepped off. The woman bent down, set her handbag on the floor and lifted a fist-sized white-furred toy breed from the center of it. It wore a red cape with Service Dog embroidered on it. As the woman straightened up, she tapped the sunglasses from atop her head into place across her eyes.

She took one step forward and, despite the disguise, saw me. And my service dog. Bling, bling: fraud phone calling. She did not board our flight. Perhaps she also saw the folly of her calculation that by carrying a few props, she could carry off being disabled and carry her pet onto the flight.

Note

On Companionship

It derives from togetherness not based on a dependency but from the joy in being together. It stands alongside communication and respect as the pillars of a strong relationship.

Service dogs may also be our companions, but companion dogs are not service dogs. A companion dog offers comfort in a stressful situation. A service dog knows what to do to get their human out of that situation.

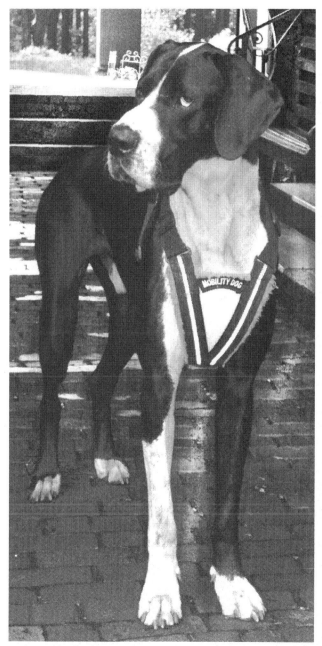

Afterword

What Next?

Live
/liv/
Verb
  - to remain alive
  - to have a life rich in experience

Of all the questions I've heard—in grocery store lines to airport restrooms—my least favorite is, *How long do those dogs live?* 'Those dogs:' Great Danes as well as 'Those dogs:' service dogs.

While I recognize that these strangers may be speaking out of kindness, warning me, trying to soften the blow of losing a partner early, I have only one response. Or, if these same strangers are making more of a statement, with overtones of *You do realize that a human's life span is longer than a dog's, especially a Dane's?*, still, the same single reply comes to mind.

My answer to their question is a question: *Do you maybe want to rethink what you just asked and not say it out loud?*

Of *course* I am fully aware that I will outlive Sir Thomas. In all likelihood, my heart will break several more times as I'll need several service dogs in my lifetime. But each of those dogs will have only one human. Me.

The gifts Tommy has given me are priceless. So, instead of focusing on the number of years in which my service dog remains alive to serve me, I've set my sights on the richness I can add to his life.

Included in the experiences are plenty of ear scratches, clean fluffies to snuggle in at night, daily reminders what a good boy he is, and a retirement plan. Yes, retirement.

Regardless of the number of years Sir Thomas is physically with me, not only does he deserve his couch time, he needs to know it's okay to age, to be creaky and not have to support my weight, to pass the vest on to a youngster while he consults as the wise elder, to know his bed will always be here even after his work is complete.

Since the application for and training of a new service dog can take two years, the process has already begun. I've already fallen in love with a pup, but this time, he's the one. There's no silver in him and he's more copper than gold. Like a shiny coin, a lucky penny. Lucky me.

Look for the more stories of life with a service dog. I'll introduce Brycen. And, no, I don't know how long I have with Sir Thomas or with any service dog. I do know that my life is richer every moment that they're in it.

Resources

There is a great deal of information on service dogs available, with quite a bit of it being inaccurate or fraudulent. Of the numerous agencies that raise and train service dogs, some, too, are legitimate organizations with knowledgeable, skilled staff and volunteers. Others are not. Here are a few reliable resources to turn to for learning more about service dogs.

The Americans with Disabilities Act (ADA)

The Americans with Disabilities Act (ADA) lays out the accessibility rights of the disabled and even defines the terms disability and service dog. It outlines the accessibility rights of the disabled person with a service dog and also lists the rights of business entities. Here is a quick reference:

ADA Regulations

Under the ADA a business or entity may ask ONLY two questions of a Service Dog Handler. They are:

1) Is the dog a Service Dog required because of a disability?

2) What work or task has the dog been trained to perform?

They may NOT ask about the person's disability, require medical documentation, require a special identification card or training documentation for the dog, or ask that the dog demonstrate its ability to perform the work or tasks.

May a Service Dog Be Removed (ADA)?

Yes. A Service Dog must be under the handler's control. It may be removed if the dog is out of control and the handler does not take effective action to control it, or if the dog is not housebroken

For more information, visit ADA.Gov or 800-514-0301 (Voice), 800-514-0383 (TTY).

Assistance Dogs International (ADI)

There is currently no federal agency monitoring the qualifications of the disabled person in need of service dog assistance or of the quality of the selection, raising and training by an agency or individual.

There is, however, a listing of trainers and service dog organizations that have met a thorough set of standards. Assistance Dogs International (ADI) is a non-profit group that provides information on the various kinds of service dogs and the work they do as well as a database that can be searched in numerous ways, such as by breed, task, state or country and disability. There is also a section that summarizes the process involved in being matched to a service dog. If it looks easier to simply go online and purchase a vest and certificate, that's because it is easier. It's also illegal and each state has differing penalties for such fraudulent actions.

Assistance Dogs At-a-Glance

Assistance dogs vary widely in breed and training. What's the difference between a therapy dog and an emotional support dog? And how are they different still from a service dog. Here's a chart that outlines the duties and training required for canines that help humans.

2-3 Years

↑

Service Dog	work for an *individual* with a *disability,*
Service, Therapy Dog	Tolerant of disturbances; crowds, noise Obedience: commands on first call
Service, Therapy, Emotional Support Dog	Socialization: Canine good citizen
Pets and Companion Dog	Some basic commands or little or no training

0-6 Months

What Is a Service Dog?

A dog individually trained to work for or perform tasks for a person with a disability

What Does a Service Dog Do?

Examples of work or tasks for which Service Dogs are trained to do for individuals with a disability:

- Guide people who are blind
- Alert people who are deaf
- Pull a wheelchair
- Protect and alert people who have seizures
- Remind people with mental illness to take prescribed medication
- Interrupt fear paralysis for a person with PTSD
- Provide support and stability for people with impaired balance

Service Dogs are essential partners to individuals with a disability and thus are permitted access to any public place the individual goes (as per ADA)

What Kind of Dog Can Be a Service Dog?

Goldens and labs are commonly seen working as Service Dogs but they are not the only breeds. Different breeds make good matches for different tasks, depending on the needs of the disabled person. Regardless of breed, a dog must display a calm, social, non-aggressive temperament to be able to work as a Service Dog.

What Other Dogs Help People?

- Therapy Dogs

Therapy dogs provide comfort, affection and happiness to people in nursing homes, hospitals, schools, therapy sessions and trauma. Therapy dogs undergo extensive training, but they are not individually trained to work for or perform tasks for people with disabilities; they are NOT Service Dogs.

- Emotional Support Dogs

Emotional Support Dogs provide comfort to an individual with a mental health disability. Emotional support dogs are not individually trained to do work or perform tasks for the person with a disability and unlike Therapy dogs, they are not extensively trained. There is no training required. They are NOT Service Dogs.

- Pets, Companions

Pets and Companions provide comfort, affection, and happiness to families and individuals. They may go through basic obedience training, but do not qualify as Service Dogs

Service Dogs Are Working Dogs

They are essential partners trained to perform tasks & work for individuals with a disability

They should not be distracted from doing their work:

Please Do Not:

- Pet
- Make eye contact
- Call out to the dog
- They do not want pets or kissy sounds; they want to do their work

About the Author

Renée Le Verrier

A childhood stroke limited Renee's mobility on her left side. Parkinson's restricts movement on her right. Sensing that she was running out of sides, Renee applied for a service dog. Sir Thomas has been by her side ever since. Trained as a balance and mobility dog, Thomas assists by providing stability and support in the house, garden, and around town.

Together, they've been to restaurants, markets, shops, hair salons, airports (including restrooms), airplanes (not including the restroom), trains, ferries (his least favorite mode of transportation), beaches, and parks.

As a team, they've presented on service dogs and handlers for hospitals, schools, police departments, Chambers of Commerce and Rotary Clubs.

To read more about Sir Thomas, visit Renee's blog:

www.leverrier.com/service-dog-parkinsons/

Made in the USA
Lexington, KY
10 August 2018